Praise for 1

"Hilarious, **humorous** – this

— *The Daily Down*

"**Two of the top humorists in America** have created a stress-free way to enjoy stress." — *Reader's Digest*

"This hilarious book will help you forget this oppressively dark period of human civilization for a good ten, eleven minutes. *The Elements of Stress* is **a perfect respite** from whichever unrelenting soul-crushing torment you're currently experiencing." – *McSweeney's Internet Tendency, editor Chris Monks*

"Not to stress you out, but BUY THIS BOOK! IT'S VERY FUNNY!! **BUY IT NOW!!!!**" — *Jack Handey, author of Deep Thoughts*

"This is **the most useful funny book** I have ever read or the other way around." – *Bob Mankoff, former Cartoon Editor of The New Yorker*

"This is **very, very funny.** Eckstein + Shaw = hilarious." – *InkSpill*

"**This book made me laugh like hell.** I was heavily sedated but it did. Looking forward to reading it more closely! Or at all."
— *Mike Sacks, Poking a Dead Frog, Stinker Lets Loose, Randy, Passable in Pink*

"If this book doesn't make you **happy-ish**, you're hopeless-ish. Thanks, Bob and Michael!" — *Ron Hauge, Simpsons, Seinfeld, The Ren & Stimpy Show*

"Bob Eckstein and Michael Shaw have penned a **humorous, easy-to-digest self-help book for our times.** They prove Erma Bombeck's adage, 'If you can't make it better, you can laugh at it.'"
— *Teri Rizvi, founder and director of the Erma Bombeck Writers' Workshop*

"Unlike with Strunk & White, I didn't stress out reading *The Elements of Stress*. In fact, I laughed out loud enough that I felt whatever the opposite of stress is. – *Decider, Alexander Zalben*

"2020 has been a menace to my stress-induced IBS. But thanks to the **hilarious** *The Elements of Stress*, I'm now only sick because I ate an entire pint of ice cream and a bag of Cheetos while reading this book."
– *Writer's Digest, Cassandra Lipp*

"Excellent jokes, a great line, prolific and occasionally profound...**you'll enjoy the book.** Bob Eckstein is rapidly becoming the Dean of American Cartooning." – *American Bystander*

THE
ELEMENTS
OF
Stress

and the Pursuit of Happy-ish
in This Current Sh*tstorm

By
BOB ECKSTEIN
&
MICHAEL SHAW

HUMORIST
BOOKS

New York

Second Edition: 2020

ISBN: 978-0-578-24105-0

Humorist Books is an imprint of *Weekly Humorist* owned and operated by Humorist Media LLC.

Weekly Humorist is a weekly humor publication, subscribe online at weeklyhumorist.com

110 Wall Street New York, NY 10005

weeklyhumorist.com - humoristbooks.com - humoristmedia.com

TABLE of CONTENTS

Introduction; *Initially, This Book Was About Gluten*

I. And God Said, Let There Be Stress

   1. History of Stress—*Past, Present, and Future—Everyone's Tense*

   2. Location, Location, Location; *Looking for Stress In All the Wrong Places*

   3. The Hilarious World of Depression

II. Great Battles of Our Day

   1. Conservatives vs. Progressives; *Red States Versus Blue States*

   2. Us vs. Mother Nature; *The Warmest Hell on Record*

   3. Man vs. Our Body; *The Depths of Despair of Jeans That No Longer Fit*

   4. Couples: *Keep Your Enemies Close and Your Exes as Far Away as Possible*

III. Handling Strife

   1. As the World Pivots: *Pivoting For Fun and Profit*

   2. Is the Box of Wine Half Empty Or Half Full; *How to Throw A Pity Party*

   3. Getting Stressed For Success

   4. Chocolate

   5. Hobbies: *The Secret of the Destressed*

   6. Say Farewell to Stress: *Top 33 Cliché Ways to Being Stressed in Descending Order*

Afterword; *The Missing Chapters*

Index

"We need you to give people a false sense of normal."

Introduction:
Initially, This Book Was About Gluten

The Elements of Style has been a beacon of wisdom for writers for the past hundred years—and it brought home the bacon for its publishers as well—selling over ten million copies. Originally written and self-published in 1919 by Professor William Strunk, Jr., on the campus of Cornell University, the "little book" was content to slumber its days away on a shelf in the special collections section of the university's library or in the campus gift-shop (The first blurb on the back cover was from Prof. Strunk himself, "Buy my book or flunk my class."). That was until *Style* was resurrected, revived, and reborn by former student and *New Yorker* literary illuminato E.B. White in 1957. His goal? To reflect the changing needs of upcoming writers and see his name on the cover with his beloved professor, William Strunk, Jr., in a super large font.

Sixtyish years later, it was only logical that this classic was due for yet another revision, and who better to take on this task than *The*

Elements of Style's most devoted disciple? Editor Lynne Truss, however, instead went and wrote the grammar bestseller, *Eats, Shoots and Leaves*, so that leaves us. And we have to eats, too. We began work on what was initially *More-or-Less Elements of Style; Now With No Index*. We wanted to not only correct typos uncovered in the previous edition ("Omit needles worts.") but usher in the new *EoS*, as we called it around the office, with the new sensibilities in line with 21st-century urban slang and the new social mores found on social media.

In the original *The Elements of Style*, E.B. White says of his co-author, "Professor Strunk was a positive man." Tested positive for what, history has never revealed, but the professor was very easy to work with, considering he had been dead for ten years when White set to work on his revision. Conversely and adversely, as work began in earnest on our new book, we were positive that neither of us had ever met a more negative person. We could not agree on anything, and we used our newly-learned urban slang to express as much. Like so many grammar textbooks, the project ended over creative differences.

Then a revelation. As we were quarantined in our respective homes, we both came to realize that our disagreements were not so much over royalty cuts or what to order for lunch, but stress. These outside forces that had nothing to do with us—the latest global pandemic, the typical political and social turmoil going on outside, our mail always being late with postage due…was all too much. We were trying to do the impossible, trying to write a well-intentioned grammar book on street slang during one of the most uncertain, tense periods in history. What the world needed was not reminders of how to make subjects and verbs agree, but how to cope with the times we live in and conjugate, literally, as a people. This country has been crying out for another life-changing self-help book that promises the moon, not a lecture on how to write gooder. Besides, what we know about grammar could fit on an em dash (but what we know about style or stress…watch out!). Now that we were no longer able to work together, we were finally able to work together separately… on the common goal of helping the world (in less than a hundred pages).

It was with this noble mission in mind that *The Elements of Stress; and the Pursuit of Happy-ish in this Current Sh*tstorm* was not so much born, but fell out from heaven at a time when we were all reaching up to the heavens for some help after the big guy dealt us such a bad hand in the way of the pandemic and a pile of other crap. It's from such pivotal points of history, like Picasso's *Guernica* during the Spanish Civil War or Warhol's *Campbell Soup Cans*, just over one year before the Kennedy assassination, that great works of art emerge—like this book. Hopefully, after reading this book, stress will roll off your back, like melons falling off a Ford F-150 pickup rolling along on the bumpy road of life. We promise you will no longer be pointing a finger at anyone again for life's shortcomings. And if not, it's your fault, and you have no one to blame but yourself. And maybe us.

Before we proceed, some SPOILER ALERTS:

This is not a diet book. For some, people eat and gain weight from stress. Others from vast amounts of carbs and refined sugar. While, when used correctly, this book will *reduce* agita. We have found that during the writing of this book we *gained* weight, so, if anything, expect to put on another five or ten pounds. This is why we recommend, ideally, running, squatting, or circuit training while reading the book. If this proves to be too difficult, have your spotter read to you. This book also contains a surprising amount of fiber. So buy two copies, one for your spotter and one to eat.

This book is not all fun and games. It is about stress! So perhaps the most effective way to approach this book is by reading under the influence. What influence is up to you—alcohol, prescription medications, edibles, Joel Olsteen, or who knows what—but we are not responsible for any reckless resolutions incurred while reading this book or operating heavy machinery. This includes but is not limited to making large purchases, getting a pet, switching political parties, drunk dialing, misguided social media posts, or changing your name. Note: this book is funnier in states where marijuana is legal. If you think you are pregnant or planning to become pregnant—congratulations!

This book is very short. Thin and short. But as they say, you can never be too thin, or rich in content. The best self-help books—on love, memory, dieting, memory, finances—ARE usually very short. Why? We've forgotten the reason why. No, wait, the reason is *The Elements of Style* was very thin. There was a reason for this. It's to absorb each lesson. Researchers and dog owners have learned that dogs handle stress better than humans. Yes, canines hide during fireworks and still have doggy worries (scientists have noted dogs twitching in their sleep), but right under our noses dogs have been compartmentalizing their stress for centuries down to bite-size liver-snack portions. *The Elements of Stress* does the same for you. Life's intractable sources of stress are served in separate, easy-to-digest chapters, like a cafeteria lunch-tray for the soul. Granted, throughout there is tough love snuck in, like cauliflower in a chocolate smoothie. But you can handle it. You're going to do great. Just keep this book within arm's reach.

Remember, you're never going to turn that page in your life unless you turn this page in the book.

THE EDITORS

Here's one of them now.

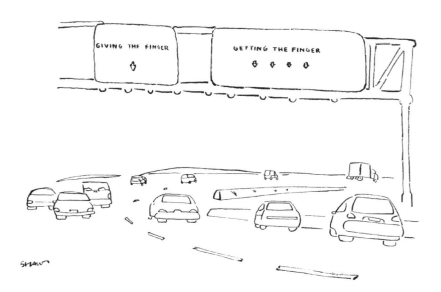

And God Said, Let There be Stress

And there was stress.

Life is stressful. Everyone's got it. Nobody wants it. Stress is unavoidable until you die, and death is just nature's way of telling us to relax, now your schedule is wide open. Unless you go to hell, which is like Stress City.

The question is why hasn't society by now successfully eliminated all of the stress in our lives? Because stress is big business. From the pharmaceutical industry, spas, cruises, psychiatrists, romantic thrillers, to fast-food joints and soap operas. Where would Ben and Jerry be without stress? Our goal is not to eliminate stress but to declutter and tidy it like Marie Kondo's sock drawer. Just roll up all that stress nice and tight and shove it in a drawer.

Let's first point out that running from stress and handling stress are two different things. Nobody can run from stress. Unless you're talking about running from murder hornets in an apiarist-recommended zigzag pattern, it's impossible to run from stress.

Instead, *address* stress. Say yes to the stress. Coping with stress has been a full-time occupation since the first creature, known as *Ichthyostega*—meaning ugly lizard with four feet— lurched out of

12

"O Lord—why art thou such a drama queen?"

the primordial flood plains of Greenland with the simple thought, "What's the worse that can happen? And what happened to my flippers?" Well, evolution failed us. How about creationism?

The next recorded incident of stress would be when the Lord woke up on the wrong side of the bed and brought forth the Great Flood.

The Lord said to Noah, "Come into the ark, you and all your household. You shall take with you seven each of every clean animal, a male and his female; two each of animals that are unclean, a male and his female; also seven each of birds of the air, male and female, to keep a species alive on the face of all the earth. And don't forget the brontosaurus—those always make me laugh. In return, I will cause it to rain on the earth forty days and forty nights, and I will destroy from the face of the earth all living things that I have made. After that, look for a weak cold front to move in over the weekend, with partly sunny skies."

Then Noah said to the Lord. "A cold front? So shall I pack a light jacket?"[1]

1 Not for nothing, if you feel you missed out on all this, The Ark Encounter features a full-size Noah's Ark, built according to the dimensions given in the Bible. It's situated now in Grant County in Williamstown, Kentucky, halfway between Cincinnati and Lexington right off I-75. Open on Sundays.

"Wait! Come back!"

Original Stress

Even Eden, that garden of paradise, was a stress-fest from Day One, or technically Day Six. It was just Adam, Eve, God, a few buzzing cherubim, and that talking snake, so what went wrong? Well, it's human nature to be curious to know what life is like outside of paradise and what's on the other side of the wall. But the real problem was God—such a micro-manager. The first helicopter parent. Meanwhile, clothes weren't invented yet, making original sin inevitable. So the real sin was launching paradise without an HR department…or developing an on-boarding procedure or dress code. Of course, getting kicked out (or as Adam frames it, "We were let go.") of the Garden of Eden was very stressful, and if only they were armed with these three principles on managing stress, it probably could have saved them both a heap of trouble.

Not to put any pressure on you—if you don't use this book correctly, you're not going to get kicked out of anything, probably. Relax—you got this. Through the simple act of reading, reflection, and modification, your brain's reaction to stress will be organized into three manageable piles: "Keep," "Fix," and "Inflict," not necessarily in that order.

"Did I remember to close the drawbridge?"

Keep

Stressors range from large and nagging—from the sun supposedly exploding in 5,000,000,000 years—to small and fleeting, like, "Where's my key fob?" In most cases, the first step, before any course of action, is deciding how much you let the source of stress affect you. That can range from illness and death to not caring at all. While not letting something bother you sounds easy enough, being apathetic goes against our ingrained DNA and our ego. Instead, everyone's day is a vast constellation of anxieties, fears, and dramas that comprise our universe or social media content. That said, the skill of ignoring most stressors is a great challenge. But one can keep and ignore some stresses if they can learn to live with them and not care. Examples of this type of stressor include essential chores, screwed-up relatives; dentist visits, In-Laws, your internet provider, taking out the garbage, triple-bogies, Thanksgiving, etc.

Fix

We need some stress to keep moving, to keep running. It was once said anxiety is a blessing in disguise. We say once because whoever said that was probably punched in the face and didn't repeat it. Stress can be a motivation to be more productive and confronting stress a call to action. That action, in turn—theoretically—would reduce or increase stress. At least you're not stuck in a rut. Keep your awareness on the stress of the

"Evolution's a bitch."

moment, not of the past or future. For instance, instead of falling into a deep depression you may first want to check all the pockets in your coats for that key fob. Can't find it? Keep looking! Even in the same pocket over and over. Now you are in a state of total stress awareness. Then you realize you didn't drive today. Stress relieved. The fact your Mini has been in the shop for three months and not fixed yet is suddenly a blessing in disguise. Some examples of stressors (that can be fixed) include: rolling up the windows next time you go through a car wash, seeing a doctor about a mysterious rash, or using an app to track things you lose, like the aforementioned key fob or your sister's handbag.

Inflict

Another stress-relieving technique is inflicting stress on others. Spreading your stress may be a form of relief at first, but this practice both spreads and mutates stress. Seldom is *Inflict* the correct approach to reducing stress but instead morphs the stressor into something bigger, Strife—blood feuds, vendettas, or marriage proposals. Grudges litter our history: from the Hatfields versus the McCoys, Red Sox versus Yankees, dogs versus cats, to potatoes or stuffing. Examples of this escalation are around us every day. The following test will illustrate that some of us don't even realize we automatically escalate most situations. Try to be honest with yourself regarding your answers.

"All booty, ill-gotten or otherwise, must be declared as income."

True or False

When you first heard about global warming, you put your fist through a wall.

Circle T or F

You readily get into fights over parking spots and have a small bat in your car.

Circle T or F

Someone you secretly don't like has a book reading. You eat chili beforehand.

Circle T or F

During the pandemic you made face masks with what you could find—coffee filters, bras, your old baseball cup, and a vintage dickie, which incidentally inspired you to craft a cheesy ventriloquist act in which you and your dummy both wore a face mask and are now booked through the summer at The Ribbon Lodge in Catskill, New York.

Circle T or F

Your score? There are no right or wrong answers. But at least you answered and it was a distraction to any current stress you may be under. Realize that stress is like buses, another one is supposed to be coming but nothing in this city works correctly.

History of Stress
Past, Present, and Future—Everyone's Tense

It didn't take long after Man invented the wheel that he got a stressful flat (despite the wheel being chiseled from stone), and even though Man had also just discovered fire, it would be thousands of years before he would use it to light a relaxing scented candle. Man couldn't catch a break.[2]

"I say we throw the damn things overboard."

And so it was for ages; The Stone Age, The Bronze Age, The Copper Age, The Middle Ages, Age of Disappointment, The Jazz Age, The New Age, The New and Improved Age (and other important ages we are leaving out for the sake of brevity). None had the luxury of what we have now, Man's most useful technological advancement, the fidget spinner. They can be purchased using a thing called a computer

---

2 While we are on the subject, why is it implied it was man who discovered fire and the wheel, and not a woman? There is no scholarly evidence or convincing cave art to the contrary. Early humans, people. It's 2020, can we use the term early humans?

or a device commonly called the smartphone with digital currency and shipped straight to your doorstep. Until this innovation, Man had only his stress balls to squeeze for relief.

Scientists found that the reason stress balls never lived up to their hype was due to one small, yet crucial, design flaw: even the very first stress balls had corporate logos printed on them, constantly reminding man they worked for *The Man*.[3] It was like the snake eating the tail of the snake, but totally different.

The best way to sum up the history of stress is that it has always been about the unknown. Nothing is more stressful than the unknown. The real results are never as horrible as what we imagine, whether it's test results or how much something costs. And not much has changed throughout civilization. "What's under the bed?" is the same as "What's in that dark scary cave?"

It's no surprise that job growth in the clairvoyant industry has always been vibrant. Palm readers, psychics, and fortune cookie writers are some of the few recession-proof occupations. Who could have seen that? They claim they did.

"Please remember past performance may not be indicative of future results."

---

3 Or *The Woman.*

"Oh, just break it anywhere."

Location, Location, Location
Looking for Stress in All the Wrong Places

Nobody can get better without locating the source of their stress. Specific stress-inducing locations in our country, like hurricane belts, tornado allies, flood-planes, earthquake faults, gated communities, and radon-soaked trailer parks are covered later in the book. This chapter explores stress found in the home. As the ancient Viking warrior, Volsunga Saga, once said, "Where wolf's ears are, wolf's teeth are near." Meaning, most accidents happen in the home. So for now, we are going to ignore the car dealerships, dentists, wolves, and other admittedly major stressors and stick close to the home.

It used to be that the living room was the most stressful room because it was where the one TV set was and where the family gathered, but it's now commonplace to have TVs throughout the house including the bathroom and she-shed. News and events are constantly being streamed into your brain through a plethora of devices and apps—from Google Glass to TikTok. The pandemic kept us from watching professional sports, which normally reduced stress. Instead there was no escaping the Situation Room and its relentless stream of stress. Blitzer, in fact, is trending as this year's most popular baby name, for both sexes. Wolf, a close second.

The last oasis left in the American home, the only room left taking a break from Breaking News, is the Mudroom. As far as anyone knows, nobody has a TV in their Mudroom. Sure, there are other dangers spread out every part of the house, like faulty gas heaters, oven cleaners, loose extension cords, heated laptops, rabid pet dog, polished floors peppered with abandoned toys, leaky microwave ovens, clogged dryer lint vents, chain saws left inside, unvetted, unstable babysitters on drugs, and vintage toasters covered with highly flammable knitted cozies, but it's the TV, surveys say, that have the most lasting influence on one's physical and mental state.

The biggest problem is, that according to a 2019 study by NAHB (The National Association of Home Builders), it's impossible to determine what percentage of homes even have a Mudroom, but our personal experience is that most homes either do not have one or homeowners prefer to call it something less-stressful sounding, like back-porch, entry foyer, three-season room, or breeze-way.

The study does reveal that the Mudroom, or Entry Foyer, averages an allocation of space in new homes of 3%. Or about 86 square feet. Yet, disproportionately, statistics show people spend 7% of their time in the home in the Mudroom, or Entry Foyer, and 87% of homeowners walk thru this room to access other parts of the house. Obviously, this cherished space should be renamed the Comfort Room. Everyone's life would have less stress with fewer rooms equipped with television. In other words, the whole country would be healthier and have less stress if new homes were designed with multiple Mudrooms.

So what if your home doesn't have a Mudroom or Entry Foyer? Your best bet is the Laundry Room—or as some homeowners call it, their Laundry Area—as the noise from the dryer can possibly drown out the news from the Laundry Room TV, or like the White House helicopter, mask our President's speeches.

For God's sake, the one place to avoid in the home, at all cost, is the Breakfast Nook. Nothing good happens there. Breakfast? In this country, the worst meal of the day. That big bowl of Lucky Charms which used to fuel a day of youthful optimism is now poison, and local morning news is the worst news on earth—no matter where you live. Home invasions, local fund-raisers for family tragedies, traffic reports, replacement window providers, varicose vein clinics—and those are just the commercials.

Turning off the TV won't help. There's all those emails or overnight tweets to soldier through. Unfortunately, this state of affairs is only going to get worse, as many reading this are in the midst of election season. It will be at the Breakfast Nook where the first ratings and poll results come rolling in. It's also where most will run into their family or spouse, some for the first time in the day. One solution can be to close off the Breakfast Nook until Election Season is over or blood pressure numbers and other vital signs are safely down.

Finally, many are wondering what is wrong with just going outside. Murder hornets.

"We need to start seeing other news sources."

"If I have to explain the joke, it's not funny."

Hilarious World of Depression

Whoever said laughter is the best medicine was probably medicated. How else does one explain the tragic history of all the great comedians who have taken their own lives? It's too ghoulish and depressing to cite the many examples of troubled stand-ups by name here, but trust us, the amount is astonishing and those who currently suffer from depression range from Jim Carrey to Pete Davidson. And who's sadder than clowns? There's even a name for the condition, Sad Clown Paradox. The only thing more depressing would be to spend the rest of this chapter explaining it.

So why doesn't having a sense of humor jive with the popularly accepted, and even scientific, understanding that laughter is a stress release? There is only one logical reason: receiving and hearing laughter does little. It's actually laughing that's therapeutic. Being funny won't help you one iota. You're probably healthier being the unfunny one of the group. When you're the funny person, that's when you have to watch out.

Don't be funny. Just surround yourself with humorous people to reap the benefits of stress relief. The good news is that it's far easier to not be very funny and just see where all the laughter is coming from than to have to perform and incite laughter. As a celebrated cartoonist and co-author once noted, "Tragedy, plus time, equals comedy. But who has time anymore?"

Being depressed is so depressing, this chapter can't come to an end fast enough. So, without further ado, here are some cartoons specifically designed to release your stress. Insensitive bar graph included.

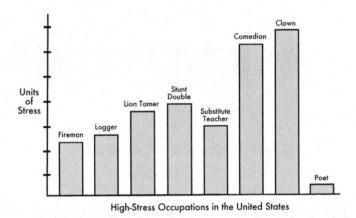

High-Stress Occupations in the United States

Earworm Ward

"First of all, there was a bee in the car."

"There goes that new-car smell."

Great Battles of Our Day

Every day you go to war. You wake up because your bladder is fighting with you and you need to use the bathroom. Without knowing it, your antibodies have been up all night flowing in your bloodstream fighting any bacteria and viruses. Your neighbor's leaf blower is going and it's only 7:30 a.m. Off to work you go to square off with your superior. Or possibly worse, the unemployment agency. But first your commute through the battlefield of your choice—whether it's the information highway in your Breakfast Nook, a highway teeming with road rage or mass transit with its stress-inducing shortcomings.

But somehow you make it to the end of the day even if it means you are clutching a pint of Very Rocky Road ice cream. The reason is resilience. And a game plan. The following chapters will address the main battles impacting our current existence. With a little future existence thrown in for good measure. A wedding planner famously told General MacArthur once, "We have seen the enemy and it is us—but mainly you."

"They should make the election best of seven."

Conservatives vs. Progressives
Red States Versus Blue States

Speaking of generals, the 18th-century Prussian General, Carl von Clausewitz once said, "War is merely the continuation of politics by other means." As a military theorist, Clausewitz (couldn't be his real name) stressed the psychological evils of war and politics but passed away before finishing his book Vom Kriege (*On War*) and its controversial last chapter on political role reversal and cosplay. Applied today, this concept could be very helpful to inter-political party households and workplaces among Conservatives and Progressives.

These groups have been at each other's throats since we got over here, but it hasn't been this bad since the Republicans were the Whig Party during the Civil War and it was the Yankees against the Confederates. A history of this grudge can be traced back in the thinly-veiled Broadway romp, "Damn Yankees," which has morphed into the current Red Sox State / Blue pin-stripe State dynamic and the second installment of the *Planet of the Apes* series.

For the first time in this nation's modern history, couples are literally breaking up over politics. Families are feuding and splintering over opposing views. Each breaking news flash adds fuel to the fire in our inner-circles, and people are not speaking to each other. It's easy to suggest just seeing the other side's views and finding common ground, but is there much common ground to be found?

The only thing clear is that the two political sides currently agree on only one thing: they both want what's best for this country and to uphold the ideals the other group had been trying so desperately to destroy. Countless editorials claim their party creates unity while the other is about creating a gridlock that seems to have no end in sight. No wonder America's blood pressure and eczema are at an all-time high.

Great thinkers and stand-ups have suggested what is probably the only realistic solution in sight: a divorce. Marriage experts now concede that ten years is a good run. The forming of this country was basically on a lark, an experiment, and we lasted almost 250 years. That's like 4,000 years in Hollywood-couple years. Anyone watching CNN and FOX on a split-screen has to agree that we have Irreconcilable Differences. We are in the middle of a second Civil War, only with less civility. And an armistice is nowhere in sight because instead of hand-to-hand combat, we're fighting finger-to-finger flame wars on Facebook and Twitter.

That said, the solution is the OPPOSITE of what the experts prescribe. What do lawyers advise in the middle of a divorce? Cut off communication. Don't listen. No contact, nothing. That's what we have to do. Stop trying to understand the other side. It's not going to happen. And stop calling them names or yelling. No more late-night drunk tweets asking them to take you back. It's over. Time to move on and lower your stress levels. Pour yourself a glass of wine and walk in the opposite direction of your computer. At least do a trial separation between politics and marriage.

"I'm just like any other politician in the race—I take my pants off one leg at a time."

"This time last year we were frolicking in the snow."

Us vs. Mother Nature
The Warmest Hell on Record

Who wouldn't want to see that Battle Royale to the death? While Man has been behaving like he's been at war with the planet since, like forever, Mother Earth has landed some blows herself in the form of very colorful, exciting natural disasters like tsunamis, earthquakes, avalanches, tidal waves, volcanic eruptions, heat waves, blizzards, colossal asteroids, and good ol' fashioned sinkholes. Now she has served up the doozy of them all, global warming, and in our corner we have the biggest sinkhole ever telling us not to worry.

What, us worry? That would be MAD. Of course, what on earth is going on is all extremely stressful for any sane person. Everyone else is crazy with optimism. We're just getting over the mother of all viruses (at least for this century) and certainly, our relationship with our environment is on the rocks if not very shaken. So you should be stirred. Installed solar panels, switched over to flimsy paper straws, and what thanks do you get? Terra farting in your face. What's the alternative?

Root against Mother Nature and donate your *Save the Planet* T-shirts to Goodwill? How come we don't see any *Save Me* T-shirts? There should be. Mother Earth can kick some serious ass.

So, since this is all about us, how do we relieve stress? There's a lifetime of advice you can try in the second half of the book—compost to throw against the wall and see what sticks—but for now let's discuss some strategy, some kind of mode of attack, or what the kids call, *activism*.

"As I said before, I can't hear a word you're saying."

Start downsizing and eliminating crap. Your primary sources of stress lead to global warming, cancer, or the Trump Administration. If we learned anything from the pandemic (by that we mean the Trump Administration), it's that our dance card is full and we need to reassess our lifestyles. Stress is caused by human activities, and staying cooped up hasn't helped. Are we human or chicken? That's why there was a Little Ice Age in Europe in the Middle Ages. Everyone stayed away from pandemics. Kept the carbon footprints down. Nobody went to amusement parks or campaign rallies. Peasants free-ranged responsibly. And everyone start moving to higher ground.

*"Just remember, if you give a hundred and ten
per cent, I get twenty per cent of that."*

DEATH, TAXES & MY UROLOGIST, DR. AARON KATZ

"This is also the warmest hell on record."

"We found this in your brain."

"There's no shooting—we just make you keep smoking."

Man vs. Our Body

The Depths of Despair of Jeans That No Longer Fit

Moving on to a battle closer to our hearts, livers, and gall bladders—the war we rage with our own bodies. As much as we hate most everybody, we hate our own bodies more. Our preoccupation with changing, fixing, tweaking, and making things relatively larger, smaller, firmer, either hairier or hairless, smoother, or more jaunty on our person is probably the biggest business in the world not counting the electronics business. Or the entertainment industry. Or finance. The point is, everyone wants to lose five or sixty pounds. Preferably without diet, exercise or disease.

But the Big Kahuna is mortality. The mortality rate remains at about 100%. Nothing is more stressful than the prospect of cashing in your chips. Take great solace in knowing that there has never been a time in history with more advanced health care, even if most of it may be out-of-network.

People died of gout in the Middle Ages (that's how Nostradamus passed away and, yes, he predicted his own death the day before). Not to mention Yellow Fever, Congestive Fever, Ship Fever, Winter Fever, Green Fever, Pringle Fever, Jail Fever, Mortification, Palsy, French Pox, Scrumpox, and Dropsy. As Shakespeare wrote in his journal—

"Another 1,500 souls hath shunted their mortal coil to the plague—black willeth again be the hot colour this fall."

These days the odds of staying alive longer (with varied and interesting ailments) has never been better. But don't despair. You've never had more control over life-choices and health. The Internet has endless information, diagnoses, and treatments, including Cyberchondria, the compulsive urge (based on unfounded escalation of concerns) to search online for illnesses and conditions.

bob

Safety has also improved. For instance, in the world of transportation and in the workplace with fewer things falling on top of people's heads. True, Gun Fever now rivals Pringle Fever as a major health-care crisis but like with many other self-inflicted ailments, we have a lot of say on how safely we can protect ourselves.

It's very Darwinian to see the behavior during a pandemic regarding the willingness of our endangered species to wear a face mask and take precautions while others feel we cannot control when "one's number is up." This eat, drink, and shoot demographic who revel in dealing with stress through reckless revelry has always embraced the philosophy that "ignorance is bliss" (Thomas Gray, 1742) attitude. And we have become the most blissful country in quite a while. If you need an explanation of that quote, then God bless you and stress is probably not your biggest problem. Though you might want to get tested for Scrumpox.

For centuries, organized religion would have us believe we even have control of the afterlife, but our choices were dubious, with all due respect to Walt Disney and Ted Williams, who each decided to freeze their heads.

Of course, you too could "pull a Walt" and scrunch down in your basement freezer and hope your widow pays the electric bills. Hard to say, pun intended, what kind of shape you will be in if medicine finds a cure for Gun and Pringle Fever, and defrosts you as this is all pretty new stuff. But as someone with some experience in time travel (once declined an invite to use a time portal to Philadelphia, 1960), here's a bit of advice when being frozen: dress in layers.[4]

---

4 Also, a good idea to buy a generator.

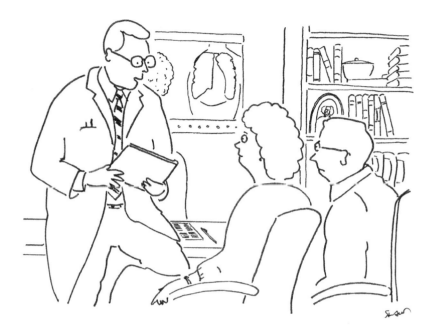

"I've identified that mysterious lump, Mrs. Feldman.
It's your husband."

Couples
Keep Your Enemies Close
and Your Exes as Far Away as Possible

A recent online survey on e-disharmony.com revealed that stress
is the number one factor in relationship disharmony. A life-partner
taking up bagpipes came in a close second. Stress in a relationship can
feel relentless because of its proximity, especially if you and that special
someone share a studio apartment. Cabin fever can transform lovebirds
into snipes. The pandemic of 2020 broke up many a couple or affair.
Long-distance relationships came to mean anything more than 6 feet
away.

But it's also the easiest stress to address, especially if you two have separate addresses. Amazingly, the solution for all relationship stress can be found within the pages of *The Elements of Style* from more than 70 years ago. What follows is a thoughtfully appropriated, verbatim application of Strunk's edicts applied to the stickiest of grammatically incorrect relationship conundrums. All we are saying is give parse a chance.

"Can we talk about this after work?"

Be Realistic

Omit needless alibis. You're not that great a catch. No one is (unless Scarlett Johansson or Colin Jost are reading this and then good for each of you for catching each other). Popular culture will have us believe that everyone else is like Romeo and Juliet and enjoying a far more exhilarating love life. They are, but are they any happier? And how did it end for them? The sooner we graciously acknowledge the final curtain call, the sooner we stop chasing the unattainable, chewing up the scenery, and accept our happy-ish fate. By focusing and appreciating the stress created by the love of your life—it's easier to move past current conflicts.

Omit the Obvious

Keep it simple. Keep it crisp. Serve the dressing on the side. Whoever said honesty was the foundation to any union was obviously never in a serious relationship. Or in a union. Today, having a significant other (even a cat) is significantly more complicated. The proof is in the pitfalls and the litter box. There are hook-up apps, emotional infidelity, sexual fluidity, and two-party marriages to contend with. Today *All You Need Is Love* would be a "missed connection" listing on Craigslist. Rule one: you know nothing.

EXAMPLE:
Instead of:
"There was a really cute person in front of me in line at Whole Foods who I think was smiling at me under their mask, so I'd like to go back there for a few hours and just see if they show up."

Use this:
"Are we out of kombucha?"

Use the Plural
As a couple, use the plural in every sentence especially when there is blame to go around. Follow this rule in the house but especially among company.

EXAMPLES:
Instead of:
"They're your friends. Why do I have to give up my Friday night?"

Use:
"We are not going bowling over our dead bodies."

Avoid Foreign Languages
Omit Esperanto. Unless you are blessed with a sexy accent, a fake accent comes off as pretentious, especially to your partner. "Ĉu vi ofte venas ĉi tien?"* does not age well. They may not have expressed so, but trust us, it's annoying. Please regard your spouse's comfort and speak in English. Though Italian is still pretty cool, even for the most *complicato* of situations.

* *"Do you come here often?"*

EXAMPLE:

Instead of:

"Da quando ti conosco la mia vita è un paradiso. Arrivederci amore mio. Ciao!"

[Since I met you my life is paradise. Farewell, my love. Goodbye!]

Use:

"Goodbye."

"Gays and lesbians getting married—haven't they suffered enough?"

Do Not Let Other Family Members Handle Your Finances

When couples are asked what their biggest problem is, the answer is invariably "finances." Most matrimonial stress stems from the old adage, "The cash is always greener." That said, never use or involve other family members to handle money or legal issues. If you don't create boundaries, that bedroom will become crowded. Some relatives require actual distances, like state borders, for social distancing. Remember to forget Change of Address cards.

EXAMPLE:
Instead of:
"You want your brother to handle this? Doesn't he still owe us all that money he invested in scented, breathable face masks?"

Use:
"I know a guy..."

"Maybe you should work from someone else's home."

Do Not Overstate

When you overstate, everything else you proclaim will be suspect in his or her mind as they will lose confidence in your judgment and your poise. Profanity is an illustration of overstatement, loss of composure, and diminishes your character.

EXAMPLE:
Instead of:
"I did not [insert preferred sexual activity], [insert current sexual partner (Adding formalities adds to the overstatement)]."

Use:
"Your friend Carol and I had buttered [air quotes] scones for tea."

Vigorous writing is concise. So is vigorous lying.

Handling Strife

Oh, let's just get on with it already.

"Jim, just put that hole behind you."

"Whatever happens, Jenkins, you'll always have your dancing to fall back on."

As the World Pivots
Pivoting For Fun and Profit

The French have 113 words for penis. And only one word for snow—neige. "Alors! Let us go outside and make a neigeman!" By contrast, the American male has only one word for his penis—*Leviathan* (which is found in the Bible and means sea monster). The French word pivot also means penis and dates back to the early 1600s from the root of dialect *pue*, meaning 'tooth of a comb.'

But we are interested in the word pivot used as a verb, meaning "to turn as if on a pivot." It was not until a diary entry in 1841 that we see the word used in this form: "Today I am pivoting from my, literally, crap job as gong farmer, cleaning out privies, to the exciting world of lath-making, doing whatever it is they do." [5]

Up until this point, *Elements of Stress* has been pondering strain and worry without providing any practical solutions. Pivoting is the big secret. Usually pivoting is just changing or adjusting one's career. But aside from professional pivoting, one must ask if they are pivoting as much as possible? Are you pivoting in your personal life? Because here

---

5 Also referred to as *gongfermors* or *gong-fayers*, was a term first used in the 15th century England to describe someone who removed human excrement from cesspits and privies. Eventually inspired *The Gong Show*.

there is more often potential for an immediate change whereas a career change requires time for training and creating opportunities. You can dump your boyfriend tomorrow. Or decide you love jazz and want to be an art lover. Let's weigh the options:

Pandemic Pivoting

Sadly, the pandemic made everyone reconsider everything. For some that meant ultimately pivoting away from loved ones who we shared unimaginable time confined together with, learning we hate each other. And hopefully, it brought some couples closer together, rediscovering the joys of pivoting. Which, by the way, was a source of stress to those having to hear how well others were doing. So you can't win.

For some, the quarantine forced us to pivot away from things we love but which are unhealthy or stupid, such as all-you-can-eat seafood buffets or doing the wave in stadiums. No doubt some of these pivots would have provided temporary relief of stress. How many of these lifestyle changes lightened the burden for you?

- Saying "No" more frequently to wedding and baby shower invites (and "Yes!" to balcony shivarees)
- Spending less time in pretentious beer gardens and instead transform your living room into an unpretentious beer garden
- Having an excuse to skip Burning Man
- Never getting out of bed
- Never returning to the gym
- Returning to the gym, but just sleeping on a sofa there
- Missing children recitals, interventions, or live support groups, and generally caring less
- Remotely going to the dentist or urologist

Many of these changes are also money-saving and will thus reduce stress levels. We call that in the stress profession, double-dipping, or multi-non-tasking.

Personal Pivoting

Change is good, and the sky's the limit as to how much one can pivot. It's a matter of deciding what in life is a stress source. The most obvious Personal Pivot is time management. Time is a commodity, and when you waste it, it incites stress. Who hasn't fallen into a bottomless Wikipedia sinkhole and spent hours learning everything there is to know about Roy Orbison for no good reason? It's easy to fall into this trap. The following is an exchange on Quora:

"Does anyone know what ADELE stands for? — *writer*"

Answer: "I love everything Adele stands for." — *some stranger you are now reading instead of getting on with your life.*

Do not confuse pondering with pivoting. Pivot pondering leads to rationalization, which generates procrastination leading to dissatisfaction, indemnification, and ultimately, hospitalization with hallucinations.

People Pivoting

Personal Pivoting blurs into People Pivoting, which is such a broad, annoying category, it deserves special attention. People Pivoting means spending more time with certain people and ditching others. How do you know when it's time to People Pivot? Has someone maxed you out? Is time with them not satisfying? You try to make them change, but they just don't get it? (It may be time to buy them a copy of this book.)

Keep pivot preferences impersonal. Choices are to be scientific, rational, and detached from judgment—how would Buddha pivot?

Environmental Pivoting

Environmental Pivoting is actually often how you People Pivot, providing an excuse to turn a smothering relationship into a long-distance relationship. As opposed to taking out the trash and never returning.

Sometimes the relationship is not with a person but a location. Living in a city, or in the suburbs or the country, affects everyone differently. Many an urbanite escaped to nature during the pandemic to be surrounded by semi-domesticated squirrels, raccoons, and bears, but the war with nature is real. Now rural America's irritants are not so much poison ivy and murder hornets but the other humans one stumbles upon in the woods, neighbors blasting out Joan Jett's *I Love Rock 'N Roll* from their jet-skis on the front porch. Environmental Pivoting is picking your poison. Would you rather wait 25 minutes for a table in Starbucks because everyone in L.A. has some deal brewing or be first in line at 5:30 a.m. for the local diner to open so you can beat the old-timers wearing red caps to a stool at the counter? This is only a rhetorical question.

The grass is always greener in someone else's yard and studies show that moving is one of the most stressful events in one's life, along with getting a divorce, losing your virginity, and going to the DMV. You can be unhappy anywhere, but you can only be happy in some places. Spending one's whole life in a hurricane belt or a flood zone is stressful and a major cause for environmental pivoting. The only one releasing stress when living on top of a major earthquake fault line is Mother Earth herself.

Spiritual Pivoting

Everyone has a God-given right to worship and fear His mighty vengeful wrath, but with so many choices out here now, there is no reason to be stuck with a deity you think is not working or you no longer like. Everyone changes in life, hopefully, and the choices you make now are not the same you made as a thirteen-year-old when you had your first communion or bar mitzvah. Worse, a current belief system can be a hidden source of stress, when it should in fact be working for you. Or at least provide a pleasant church-supper once a month in the basement.

Religions are like insurance policies, you don't think you need it until something horrible happens. And when was the last time you went to confession? Or got a live voice on the line with your insurance company? So, shop around for the best deal and work with an agent you like, someone who will return calls. Weigh the deductibles. In religion that equates to the company you will have to keep. Find a plan that's right and make it part of the arsenal in fighting stress.

"Would you rather be attacked by a horse-size duck or fifty duck-size horses?"

Involuntary Pivots

Granted, not all pivots are under one's control and can ratchet up stress. As someone who has been fired, dumped, and had to evacuate due to an impending hurricane, on the same day, the only thing left is perspective. Forced pivots can be demoralizing at first, but being honest in these dark hours is the best defense—

- Didn't that job suck anyway? How badly do you need disposable income anyway?
- Were things ever going to work out between you two, especially after the last election?
- Isn't it nice to finally cash in on all that home insurance you invested in?

Pivoting is the new life hack, but it can also be a big step. Start with weekend pivoting and work up to full-fledged pivoting. With enough pivoting, you'll even convince yourself you're being productive.

"*My, this Cabernet pairs well with your parents and
the four Martinis I had at the bar.*"

"More Château de Costco?"

Is the Box of Wine Half Empty or Half Full?
How to Throw a Pity Party

De-stressing can be as simple as changing your state of mind. One's perspective of any situation can be solved with a simple, "Whatever." Are you a half-full or half-empty type of person? Perhaps it would help if you graduated to a box of vino? Maybe the answer is to throw a pity party. And if it's your pity party, you can cry if you want to.

There's nothing sadder than drinking alone. If you are not yet ignoring the well-advised advice to avoid bars, then it's time for a Zoom Pity Party. If not done properly, a party can just add to the pity and be quite stressful, so let's look to the New Testament for throwing a good pity party:

"Give…wine unto those that be of heavy hearts….some small sharing plates would be nice, too."

— Letter from RuPaul to the Kardashians

While the Bible makes no mention of computers or Zoom, wine and multitudes weigh heavily. The following is an interview with wine expert, Father John of Holy Moses of Hamlin, Pennsylvania.

Elements of Stress: *What do you recommend for a Zoom pity party in 2020 A.D.?*
Father John: Nothing pairs with stress quite like wine. Whiskey is risky, beer too austere. But wine? Calamity and cabernet. Paranoia and Pinot. The elegantly dry, yet spicy floral and fruity hints of an Alsatian Reisling is perfect for savoring someone else's misfortune.

EoS: *What is your stance on box wine?*
Father John: Lugging the Big Glug Box 'O Wine at Costco to my car is quite a workout and requires the assistance of altar boys and Brother Jim. So logistically, I have to coordinate everyone's schedules.

EoS: *What about the wine itself?*
Father John: The wine is fine. Somewhere between a house wine and a House of the Lord wine, with hints of frankincense and myrrh.

EoS: *Good enough for Jesus?*
Father John: Ahhh, the savior of souls and wine. Probably not.

EoS: *So then, WWJD—What would Jesus drink?*
Father John: Jesus…Best guess, a hardy Cab. Something strong of spirit to pair with the weak of flesh. I'm not suggesting he wouldn't choose a box wine. He was a bit on the cheap side. At the Last Supper he said, "Take this check, all of you, and split it."

EoS: *Was there wine when he produced baskets of fish to feed the multitude?*
Father John: Actually, guests had a choice of fish or chicken.

EoS: *How important is wine to relieving stress?*
Father John: Very. I speak from personal experience. I have two drinks a day. Three, if I have MSNBC on. The average ancient Roman citizen chugged down three liters a day, and they were one of the least stressed civilizations in history. That's a fact. I think.

But you want to relieve stress? Hope. Hope and love. Man must have hope and love in his heart. And I walk three miles to clear my head every day if I don't have a hangover.

"I'm getting earthy overtones of guilt, with just a hint of sexual frustration."

*"Meet your sales numbers this month, Feldman, and
you can have your head back."*

"Can everyone clearly fear me?"

Getting Stressed For Success

Maybe we're going about this in the wrong way. Instead of running away from stress, perhaps the solution is to run right at it. Exploit the sucker and join the millions who have found ways to monetize it (for example, the sequel to this book has already begun). Whether it's the drug companies or spa owners or liquor stores or the psychiatric field, stress is Big Business. So without further ado, let's discuss how to capitalize on stress;

Join
Become a member of the community profiting from stress and support stress related activities.

Validate
Start with yourself. Try this simple exercise. From here on in, have everyone you meet and befriend call you "Doctor." Immediately, you will enjoy how wonderful it is to be addressed this way. I for one can tell you, it's a true stress reliever, and it's barely illegal. Whether these

new connections are from your workplace or a cocktail party, your new friends will never follow up to see whether you earned a doctorate. Okay, one or two people may Google you and ultimately learn you are not a doctor, but think of how many who wouldn't bother to check on this and would be impressed. If you happen to be a real doctor, our sincere apologies.

Mobilize

It's time to go shopping. Trust starts with first impressions, and dressing to impress is the way to success with stress. The benefits are twofold as clothes shopping is scientifically an effective stress reliever. Remember to keep your receipts. This is all tax-deductible as a business expense now that you turned shopping into Big Business. When you go out of business, you can return the clothes.

Prey

Victims pray, doers prey. Think about that awhile. Now that you know so much from *The Elements of Stress*, you have a full understanding of the Supply and Demand dynamics of the highly stressed American. List your passions, and then throw that list away. Come up with two or three businesses you could start in your area fitting the needs of your stressed neighbors.

So start brainstorming and go with the one you come up with the niftiest name for, like a fun take-out place:

The Unintentional House of Panic

Kentucky Freud Chicken

Uncontrollably Shake Shack

Taco Hell

McDemic's

Yips!

Financing

Congratulations, it's time for a bank loan you have no intention of paying back. It's important that you have this attitude, otherwise, if you have that loan hanging over your head, it's only going to stress you out terribly.

Prescription AntiDepressant Ice Cream

DOUBLE DIVORCE

Vincent Van Cookie Dough

Really Rocky Road

CHUNKY MELANCHOLY MONKEY

new! new!
Screwed Up Childhood Mocha Swirl!

bob

Chocolate

There are many books on managing stress which blabber ad nauseam on long-term solutions and strategies. You may have even heard of the N.U.T.S. principle; Novelty, Unpredictability, Threat to your ego, and Sense of control. But this is the only book that is going to tell you what you want to hear. That the answers are at your disposal, and in many cases, already in your house. You don't have to go out and spend tens of thousands of dollars on psychotherapy–the financial burden and anxiety from unrealistic expectations just create new stressors. The solutions are right under your nose and surprisingly affordable. You are about to be rewarded for your patience getting this far.

Chocolate

What did the world do before chocolate? If you study the advancements in cacao drinks and confectionary, you'll see the correlation between chocolate and all the most stressful events in world history. The Great Irish Famine was around 1847…when the chocolate bar was invented. It was during the Great Depression that Nestle began processing a quarter-million pounds of condensed milk a day. (Stock analysts have since relied on chocolate consumption as a market indicator.) During the Revolutionary War, soldiers were often paid in chocolate instead of money. In World War II, Hershey Bars and Lucky Strikes were a stable of every G.I.'s rations and balanced meals, no doubt to help cope with the rigors of war. This sweet treat has always been a balm for stress and a boon for dentists. Recent reports indicate that chocolate sales and waistlines have exploded during the COVID-19 pandemic.

The same can be said for ice cream. Look at the most horrible times of our planet's history, a pint of ice cream was never far away.[6] There's always been a strong tie between ice cream and the mental-health industry. Many studies have been conducted on ice cream and its effects on one's serotonin levels. Ben & Jerry were psychiatrists. Mr. Softee was originally a sex therapist. This is why a hot fudge sundae, while probably the healthiest food in one's diet, has been long considered by therapists as a symbol of repressed stress they call a "Hot Freud Sundae."

Stress Balls

Don't throw out your stress balls. Just because these are often free giveaways at very stressful business conventions, don't underestimate their value. Try squeezing a stress ball once a day for five minutes,

"Love, L-U-V, love the new stress balls!"

---

6 The children's ditty was originally, "You scream, I scream, we're all screaming in abject terror for ice cream and can't stop screaming!"

increasing the duration by one minute each day. After a couple of months, you should have worked up to over an hour. Luckily, stress balls are such a common form of swag that you probably have eight or nine stress balls hidden away somewhere in your house already. If that is indeed the case, leave your stress balls out in the open for easy access. Keep one near the desk, one at home, one in the car. Some people have been known to place a stress ball somewhere on their person.

M•st•rb•tion

A delicate subject, difficult to discuss and for some, difficult to do. That said, without getting into the how's, when's, where's, or how many times, and focusing on the whys, this is another item on this list you should be able to find in your home already or wherever you go. Excellent as stress relief; as my Uncle Ed declared, "It's the only thing that gosh-darn computer is good for." But doctors knew, all too well, the benefits of this aerobic exercise way back in Victorian times, when patients scheduled monthly doctor visits to address hysteria, which "symptoms included headaches, epileptic fits, and very coarse language." Pelvic massage was the only answer. Men have known this since way back in prehistoric times. The curvaceous statue, Venus of Willendorf, was probably mass-produced for men and hidden under their mattresses. The beautiful Narcissus was the Greek God of self-love and had clear skin and low blood pressure, no doubt from low stress.

Binge-Watching

Binge-watching dates back to the Roman times, starting when the Colosseum tried doubleheaders and matinees. We're not suggesting you need to go all *I, Claudius* but to safely binge. We are lucky to live in an era when there are so many options to binge watch—in the Middle Ages, their only options were puppet shows or beheadings. In the early 20th century, binge-watching meant staring at the facial ticks of your immediate family as you all listened to the radio. But the main thing was it achieved relaxation. Today there's no excuse if you can't find something to help you become ~~brain-dead~~ stress-free.

"Of course, it's tangy—that's our compost bucket."

Hobbies
The Secret of the Destressed

> *"A lot of people laugh at it being a silly hobby, but it's a wonderful hobby."*
>
> —Rod Stewart speaking to the BBC

If you aren't aware of Sir Rod's secret hobby, there are no spoilers here. What's most important is that it's a wonderful hobby.[7] Fellow hobbyist Oprah Winfrey seeks a state of mindful flow with her spiritual center. Yes, that's a hobby.[8] But even if you're not Sir Rod or The Mighty O, you too can have a creative enough hobby to stress you out of your current stressful state.

Creative hobbies increase happiness, empathy, and make you more interesting at parties. Up to 25% of Americans surveyed claimed to have creative hobbies—baking, gardening, fancy cookin', and DIY crafting. Of that group, .01% claimed "survey-taking" as their creative

---

7   It's model trains, if you must know.
8   Plus, she reads books.

hobby. I guess it could be if you consider lying a creative hobby or have political aspirations. This raises the question, though, as to not only what qualifies as a legit hobby but how to make sure your leisure pursuit does not become stressful.

The answer is two-fold: 1) any extracurricular activity can be a creative hobby with some imagination, some extra savings, an Instagram account, and elbow grease, and 2) proper attitude can assure relaxation. Don't cry if your sourdough loaf doesn't rise. Stress has always played a role in leisure activity. To note, periods of strife have produced new, unique hobbies. If we look at the top hobbies of the Great Depression (in no particular order):

"No, but I can tell you the meaning of whole or term life insurance."

1. Food scrapping (later responsible for delectable Mulligan Stew [9])
2. Train travel (preferably inside and not underneath the boxcar)
3. Camping (with 300 of your closest friends next to the railroad track)
4. World War II

---

9 Meat, potatoes, vegetables, and whatever else can be found or stolen. From *The Better Hobo and Someone's Else's Garden Cookbook*.

"I brought my own bag."

Other hobbies can be traced to stressed-induced epochs, if you go back further in history. Favorite prehistoric hobbies included:

1. Trying not to be eaten by giant animals
2. Trying to eat a smaller animal
3. Campfire songs following the discovery of fire
4. Cave painting and portraiture

Even Adam and Eve, inspired by their rocky start, shared a hobby and took up cooking for survival, preparing delicious meals like Brimstone-Seared Serpent and Forbidden Apple Brown Betty.

Ask any stressed-out Hobby Lobby manager, there's nothing like taking up a hobby to add even more stress in your life. Pursuing a hobby creates so much stress, that returning to the mundane stresses of day-to-day life, such as the current political, economic, cultural, or existential crisis of the moment, seems like a vacation from your stress-filled hobby. That's why people seek out stress-laden adventures certain to cause permanent damage to both themselves and their family—like climbing Mt. Everest or going to Disney World.

"One day Son all this will be yours."

This year, the most popular hobbies were, starting with the most creative and thus best stress-relieving activities to the least:

Political grandstanding

Food porn/making bread

Thinking you can sing/Instagram

Jigsaw puzzles/figuring out what cords and chargers go with what

Running in place

Walking in place

Sleeping in place

Listening to your neighbor's music/arguments

Remote spear-fishing

Zoom stand-up

Online gambling

TikTok

Tic Tacs

Erotic needlepoint

Video-gaming with completely age-inappropriate strangers

Telemarketing from your window

Tweetstorm chasing

Hoarding stuff

Staycations

Facebook

"No one said we couldn't eat the snake."

"That Timmy's a real trouper—he's playing with a sprained ankle and head lice."

The Elements of

Say Farewell to Stress
Top 33 Cliché Ways to Being Stressed (in Descending Order)

You are about to finish the soon-to-be bestseller, *The Elements of Stress*. Don't be stressed by this. There's more. Stress, that is.

Surely, one or two of these chapters seeped into your mind, enlightening you and lightening your load, and no doubt if you have faithfully read the preceding chapters, you're probably not feeling any stress at all. You're probably asleep. And that's fine. You need your rest.

We will leave you with these parting words of wisdom: People will tell you how to be happy but then turn around and go on and on about their own stress. Our advice? Don't listen to anyone, especially self-help writers. Don't fall for clichés and cheesy metaphors.

But if you must…

"Is the Itsty Bitsy Spider obsessive-compulsive?"

We were all put on this spinning rock, fashioned to do something. Your place in the universe is in some queue, somewhere, and you just need to make sure you're in the right line. Here's where a North Star comes in, a fancy way of saying your mission statement—your passion or dogma you keep going back to for direction and decision-making no matter how much the crazy world around you is changing.

Hopefully, by this time, you know what your North Star is. Or maybe a part of you knows, but you never really contemplated this before. If you haven't got a clue, go find out why you're here. Ask around. Ask your family and friends. Ask your doctor or sponsor. Ask your parole officer, teacher, or priest. Someone here must know and can tell you.

So whether it's singing at Carnegie Hall or cleaning out horse stables, do that. Gong farming? Don't push it. Whether it makes you happy or even if it makes you miserable. Do whatever it is you think your North Star is, and make it your mission to find some joy in it. You don't even need to be the best at it…just be the best you.

And whatever stress you may be going through during this troubled period, remember time heals all wounds. As every proctologist says, "This too shall pass." This year especially has certainly been a take-

"The bad news is that you have an unknown disease.
The good news is that it will be named after me."

home test. And we won't specify what year so that whenever you pick up this book you think we are talking about that year. For those of you reading this in the year 2525, we certainly hope man and woman have survived.

Yes, we live in a competitive country...and a country of drama queens and Burger Kings. Everything has to be either the best, the worst, or a whopper. In this country, everyone insists on having it their way. Living in a cliché is stressful. Why is it every election is the most important in the country's history? Is it? Not everything has to be boiled down to a Top Ten list.

<u>Top 33 Cliché Ways to Being Stressed (in descending order)</u>

1. Being squished by a giant monster, excluding if you live in Tokyo or New York

2. Falling down a well, and your faithful collie is at the vet

3. Being struck by lightning down in that well (really, is your luck that bad?)

4. Being stranded on a tiny island with only one palm tree and not finding it funny

5. Contracting a bizarre disease named after you

6. Contracting a bizarre disease and having it named after your doctor

7. Actually being in a situation where you have to find that needle in the haystack

8. Binge-watching *Meet the Press*

9. Being hit by a car while running from murder hornets

10. Never winning the lottery ($10 weekly minimum)

11. Winning the 100,000,000 Iranian Rial in the Persian Pot O' Gold Lottery *(Current exchange value in U.S. dollars: $2,375.01)*

12. Dropping a foul-ball because you *nonchalanted* it and didn't use both hands

13. Then being taunted on the jumbotron by 15,000 cardboard cutouts

14. Being born in a Waffle House

15. Being left in a Waffle House in lieu of a tip

16. Hair loss

17. Genital hair loss

18. Living to be 125, through 3 pandemics

19. And your kids still haven't moved out of the basement

20. Graduating college in nine years

21.   And then becoming a stand-up

22.   Alien abduction

23.   Alien seduction

24.   Any family intervention and/or Thanksgiving

25.   Lost weekend

26.   Lost weekend on a spaceship

27.   Imperfect March Madness bracket

28.   Hecklers on *Poetry Night*

29.   *Shark Tank* appearance in an actual shark tank

30.   Finding a four-leaf clover in your salad

31.   Finding a fourteen-leaf clover in your salad at a favorite Chornobyl bistro that usually gets glowing reviews

32.   Never reaching The End

33.   The End

Professor William Strunk and E.B. White advised novice writers in their classic, *The Elements of Style,* not to lean too heavily on clichés. So with that, we put down our pens and rest on our laurels.

bob

Afterword
The Missing Chapters

You did it. You, and by you, we mean we, made it through this year. It would be nice to think that life now will be a breeze — but breezes are like buses, there's always another breeze and instead pleasant, it's too often the whiff of White Castle or Category 3 hurricane coming your way. Likewise, there will always be traffic and rubberneckers of the world gawking at some accident on the highway. We are never so much concerned for the health and welfare of those poor drivers in the accident (unless one of them is you), but instead excited by the sight of open highway beyond the stacked smoldering automobiles. You just passed the bottleneck. You finished *The Elements of Stress* and the open-road beckons.

Of course, we helped tremendously. We eliminated four major chapters from the text that now you don't have to read and kept this book considerably shorter (and less expensive). Without that massive editing, you would still only be halfway through the book. You would still be in that bottleneck. Granted, the chapters weren't very good and the decision to cut them was easy.

Chapters Agone
First, there was *"Declaring the War on Stress."* As Prussian General Carl von Clausewitz examined earlier in the book, war can help one be more politically active and raise our awareness of stress. *"Taking it to the stress"* as we in the stress business and activists like to say. However, recently, revolting in the name of stress has had to take a backseat to all the really good reasons protesting was voted one of the Top Five Popular Outdoor Activities. The chapter included some obligatory attempts at humor through slogans for banners with predictable puns, dotted the angry landscape but you're not missing much. "Down With Blood Pressure," "I AM STRESSED, Hear Me Roar," and "Put Down Your Signs."

The next chapter cut was *"Flight or Fight...or Flop."* Flight or fight triggers an acute stress response, a hormonal reaction but we uncovered a third reaction scientists missed: Flop, as in flop sweat. Like when you sweat emotional toxins out of you in hot yoga or if you are a comic bombing on-stage.

"Consider the possum. No fighting, no flighting, just flopping. Or the stress of any creative venture—a movie, play, or piece of fine art that is failing—it flops..." Imagine 80 pages of this.

Family Holiday Pain Chart

No pain. Experiencing zero discomfort. You would not be entirely wrong to call this a party.

Mild discomfort. Conversation is moderately easy. Of course, the evening is young. Wait, my cousin Carl is coming over to me. Bet he says something asinine.

Tolerable pain. The initial pain is not so strong that I feel I have to leave immediately but more of an annoyance, like a pebble in my shoe. Key to surviving these functions is to avoid everyone, or at least constantly circulate so you're a moving target.

Moderate pain. Like sharp heartburn or stepping on a lawn rake. Conversation is challenging but able to pretend I'm listening to others. Why is my 16 year old niece dressed like streetwalker? At least she's working which is more than I can say for most of the deadbeats in this room.

Severe pain. The boredom is so intense I decided to eat my way through a tray of bruschetta. I'd do anything for a text message right now. I may even have to go over and talk to Uncle Lou.

Strong, deep pain. The next person who tells me I look like I put on weight is going to get a cocktail weenie shoved up their nose.

Don't ask.

In the corner of the room breathing into a paper bag. The only reason I showed up here is so I'd have something to talk about on Monday with my therapist.

Very difficult. Similar to the DMV or being attacked by killer bees. I cannot even look at a pain chart. Wait, let me put my fist through that number 9 level pain. Worst baby shower ever.

No conversation is possible. Full effort is required from me to not lash out. I want to legally change my name and enter a witness protection program so that loved ones can't find me. The pain knowing I'll never get back this time, from a scale of 1 to 10, is a 38.

"*Homeopathic Approach to Stress*" was a painful chapter to cut. But we didn't have much choice. It added 370 pages to the book, and we had only gotten to the part about handling micro passive aggressions that become major stresses in life. We had hoped to discuss acupuncture in the chapter—as many of you know, there are many types; there are needles, hot rocks, cupping, hanging upside down and, being hooked up to electrodes…and maybe some of those are not actually acupuncture.

Speaking of which, we haven't talked before about herbal teas for anxiety. And we're still not. As for meditation for reducing stress, it's very controversial as to whether sitting still for 90 minutes is restful or gives you agita thinking about everything you still have to get done in the day. Having your limbs fall asleep is a nuisance in your twenties, but, as you get older, getting rid of pins and needles can last hours, if not days—if, *if* you are able to get out of your meditating position. But if you must meditate, we have some recommendations. Meditate instead in an upright sitting position. Like driving a car, during a work meeting, on ride at an amusement park, at mealtime, or while on the toilet. Limit the time you meditate to five minutes, tops. If it's not working for you by that time, you're one of those people it's never going to work for. Pivot to expensive homeopathic drops and supplements after trying placebos first. Right now the latest trend are singing chiropractors help you find your Chaka Khan and balance your pelvis; all great stress reducers. Make sure you go to a *licensed* singing chiropractor.

There was a fourth chapter eliminated but all we can remember is it had something to do with Pennsylvania.

"*Take me to your Chick-fil-A.*"

Looking Ahead to Future Stress

As renown Dr. Anthony Fauci famously said, "Those who cannot learn from history are Zoomed to repeat it." So how do we keep from repeating future stress? More importantly, can future stress be avoided? First, there's the immediate future, and in the arena of stress, the biggest headache coming your way is your next family get-together. While everyone's situation is very different, there is one common dominator we all will be sharing: stress. That next Thanksgiving, or holiday or family event will indeed be stressful. How could it not? We've got months of simmering political-charged grief and emotions percolating, and you're twenty pounds overweight now and your second cousin owes you pre-pandemic money from his failed holiday tour business.

So how do you ace your first major stress test? By proper prepping. Start a Stress Journal. From here on in, you are going to maintain and monitor your stress in a journal you have to take everywhere. That will stress you out enough that you will forget what you were stressed about to begin with. Start by rating your stress experiences. Let's say, for example, you are going to a gender reveal party—and no one is pregnant. Or an intervention/wedding combo for your niece. Use this pain chart to accurately gauge levels of possible discomfort. This growing self-awareness will have you subconsciously avoiding key people and situations that give you the most stress.

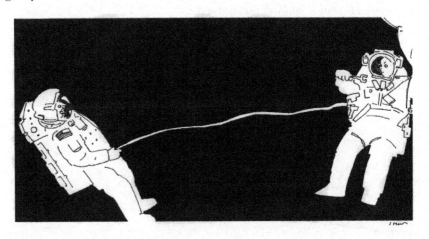

"There! I'd say that's about six feet."

"The new Agita! No driver, no brakes, no steering wheel...nothing to worry about but fear itself."

Well, what about *future*, future stress? Not stress measured by moments but the "big picture stress." Having solved global warming earlier in the book, complete with a plan to accommodate the prospect of an inhabitable planet, it leaves us with the real elephant in the garage: driverless automobiles.

Nothing is more stressful than imagining a world made up of only driverless cars (except lawyers). It would be remiss to get on the exit ramp of *The Elements of Stress* without first putting on our hazard lights about this pressing problem. It's a question of safety and fears, both real and perceived. An amended driving test would be the solution, and we have included a first rough draft. If everyone would now just take a moment to write their government representative and present them with the following test to put into legislation, it would save us all a lot of grief and stress.

State Driver's Test For Owners Of Driverless Cars

(Test du conducteur d'État pour les propriétaires de voitures sans conducteur)

The following test would be administered for those obtaining the new Class X driver's license, which is for vehicles without a driver and/or ejector seat.

1. When approaching pedestrians who are walking on or crossing the roadway, you must...

- o   pray for their lives

- o   grab the wheel and steer into hedges

- o   close your eyes and hope for the best

2. Which of the following statements are most true about driverless cars?

- o   You can't believe this is happening

- o   You cannot BELIEVE this is happening

- o   You always thought flying cars would come first

3. You arrive at an intersection at the same time as another vehicle. There are no traffic signs or signals–not that it would matter. Your car should...

- o   speed up and go through the intersection

- o   slow down and yield to the vehicle on the right

- o   You have no idea, but can't wait to see the expression on the other driver's face when they see no one is driving your car

4. Do you need to use headlights anymore?

o   Not really

o   Whenever you wake up and realize it's nighttime

o   When signaling to UFOs

o   If your GPS doesn't work and you find
     yourself in a mineshaft

5. A police officer directly behind your vehicle asks you to pull over. Your fancy-shmancy car is confused and speeds up to avoid contact. A chase ensues at ever-higher speeds. Cars nearby careen over guardrails and/or launch into the air, exploding into balls of fire as your car weaves through traffic with the cruiser in hot pursuit. You...

o   decide now would be a a good time to put on your
     seatbelt

o   you add this to that screenplay you've been working on

o   make the best use of your hands-free time to Google
     "lawyer"

o   shrug your shoulders out the window and point to the
     empty driver's seat

"It followed me home—can we keep it?"

6. What effect might drugs have on your driving?

o   Somewhat helpful

o   Very helpful

o   You don't even think about getting into one of those things without being heavily mediated

7. Your car is approaching a yellow light. You should...

o   beg your car to slow the f—- down!

o   text your car to "Slo the f—- down!"

o   select the "Slow the F—- Down" button after quickly uploading the iPanic app onto your phone

o   jump from the vehicle

8. You see an old high school friend in the vehicle in the next lane.

o   You duck down behind the backseat

o   You climb over the front seat and slam on the horn, only to have you car speed up like a bat out of hell

o   You pretend you're having sex

9. The legal age for a driver's license for a driverless car is...

o   85 yrs old

o   4 yrs old

o   [your age here]

10. The best part of a driverless car is…

- o   sitting where you want

- o   impressing dates

- o   not having to parallel park

- o   no longer being responsible for your car's accidents

11. The worst part of a driverless car is…

- o   running over small pets

- o   having no idea where you'll arrive

- o   confusion at fast-food drive-ins

- o   draw bridges

"You realize you're just honking at driverless cars, don't you?"

The takeaway here is it's never better to be alone…especially on the freeway in a 2,000 lb. motor vehicle hurtling at 65 mph with no driver. All stress is easier with someone by your side to drag them down with you as pain loves company. So take the wheel of the car and don't make your designated driver a robot or crash test dummy. Instead find someone to be miserable with.

"Gus, just keep them coming–I have a driverless car."

"If you love what you do, you never work a day in your life."

"Personally, I fail to see the humor in this situation."

"Can we tweet about this in the morning?"

How To Ease The Baby Shower Into an Intervention

"As a bonus, someday we'll name a major sports team after you."

"From where I stand it doesn't look like any of them are evolving."

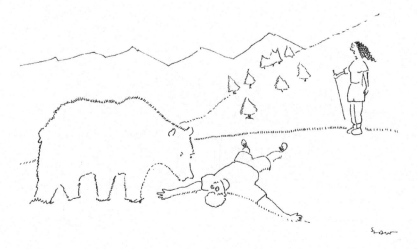

"They can sense fear of commitment."

"Tell me, Jake, tell me this was just a reenactment."

"I recommend hipster replacement therapy."

On the eighth day The Lord knocked out the rings
of Saturn which he had totally forgotten about.

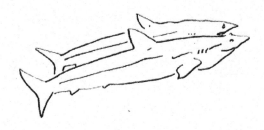

"Now, Herold, you know eating those always give you the shits."

*"How do you expect people to believe in you
when you don't believe in yourself?"*

Index

1957, 22
2526, 25-26
5,000,000,000 years from now, 3
address cards, 56
allergies, 125
amusement parks, 23
address cards, 81
algae, 44
algebra, Δ
bagpipes, 78-85
bald spots, 192
banana, 45-48
    bad, 46
    peeling, 47
    slipping, 45
    split, 48
banjos, 101
basement, 302-303
dark, 302
flooded, 302
inspection, 303
musty, 302
packed, 303
son living in, 415
termites, 302
Bikini Atoll, 1946
Black, Back In, 67
black cat, 24
Black Adder, 18
black, fade to, 00
Black Friday, 27th
Black, Lewis, 73
black mold, 56
bladder woes, 278-292
Blitzer, reindeer, 77
Blitzer, Wolf, 465
book reviews, 671
bone spurs, 11
boulder, 26
Boulder, Colorado, 88
Bronte, Branwell, 155
bugles, 90
cabbage, 103

carpet stains, removing, 405
carpetbagging, 48
cats, 160-173
missing, 163
with Irish names, 168
McCheshire Cat, 168
McCuddles, 168
McSorely's, 168
McPedigree, 168
McWhiskers, 168
McLitter, 169
McFluffy, 168
Cat O'Ninetails, 169
Cat O'Strophic, 169
cesspools, 501
clogged, 502
dreams, 502
falling in, 503-509
chicken, 3-5
crossing road, 4
free-range, 98
little, 3
clowns, 12-303
    fear of, 45
    send in, 46
    sad, 89
coughs, 11
drops, 13
elbow crook, into, 12
    fake, 14
    nagging, 15
    turn head and, 18
    whopping, 17
crashes, 133
computer, $
stock market, $$
sugar, 78
water skiing, 4U2C
deadlines, 0
disappointment, 1-72
DMV, 56
    hours, 56
    lines, 56
double faults, 15-40

Doug, 1
drunk, 68
date, 10
fans, #1
hecklers, 100s
late night robocall, 1-800
test, 2 + 2
uncle, 6
Zooming, 60 mins
dry root, 41
earthquakes, 167
elections, 2020
enemas, 190
excess gas, 4
Facebook, 233
fitting room, 23
bathing suits, 25
Cathy, cartoon, 26
mirror, 26
sticky door, 26
Flintstone, Fred, 1962
Florida, 34
The French, 18
    Vive le fromage!, 1870
    Vive Jerry Lewis!, 2017
garage door openers, 88
    repurposing into home gyms, 89
    repurposing for lifting a dead body, 89
see Scream
Garfield, 1 star
ghosting, 72
hang gliding, 101
hanging out, 90
Hollywood, 1940s
honking, 56
hurricane belts, 38"
hurricane recipe, 5
inside straights, A, K, J, 10, 4
Izzard, Eddie, 78
    Fishtybuns, Kringelbert, 503
    Humperdinck, Engelbert, 221
    Slaptyback, Engelbert, 4

Zindledack, Dindlebert, %$&!
Jerry, and Ben, 33
Jerry, and Dean, 34
Jerry, and Tom, 611
Journey, 222
kale ice cream, 5
Kardashians, 8
   Ru Paul's letter to, 112
killer bees, 68-91
Kondo, Marie, 31
ladders, 13
Las Vegas, 1905
   Viva, 1906
leaky pipes, 56
   puddles, under, 18
Lifetime Movie Network, 82
   death by frying pan, 82
   staircase, pushed down, 83
long lines, 372
long nails, 10
long-winded, 24-7
Long-winding, 66
   road, 81
losing, 89
Lucky Charms, 4
Lucky Strike, 256
Metric system, 000
   how to calculate, #
mimes, 3
   how to incapacitate, 3-7
Mother bears, 3
   how to ingratiate, 4
mudrooms, 178
   how to decorate, 179
murder hornets, 910
   how to escape from, 911
mysterious rash, 36
   how to scratch, 37
Nature, Mother, 188
   how to fool, 199
parking spots, 11
   how to find, 1 pm
parking tickets, $150

how to fix, $210
passwords, ••••
   how to forget, 64+
Poetry Night, 8-11 pm
   how to avoid, 23 skidoo
poison ivy, 13
   how to avoid, also, 411
rentals, 20
roadies, 10-4
roadkill, 187
road rage, $#%!
root canal, 68
scratches, 7
second degree burns, 119
sinking, 61
Situation Room, 78
shots, 45-49
   big, 45
   cheap, 45
   long, 45
   mug, 45
   pot, 45
   rim, 45
   slap, 45
   snap, 45
   Tequila, 45
smells, 16
   Like Teen Spirit, 17
Space Force, 2035
   crashes, 21
stock market, 19
   crashes, 29
thorn, 6
removal from lion's paw, 8
traffic jam, 32
travel bans, 50
Triple-bogies, 8
tripping, 420
varicose veins, 90
Village Green Preservation
Society, 1968
   Monica, 46
   Thunder, Johnny, 47

Walter, 56
warning lights, 72
   blinking, 72
water beds, 69
   leaking, 121
water boarding, 007
   administering, 0
weevils, 14
   (see zyzzyva)
Williamsburg Open Mic, 2017
Winfrey, Oprah, 20
winter itch, 12
zyzzyva, 14
   (also see weevils)

Other books by Messrs. Eckstein and Shaw

(pending)

Haiku for the Hysterical

Elements of Stress II: Return of Strife

Remind Me in an Hour, Remind Me Tomorrow

The Joy of Schtick: The Timeless Guide to Joke-making

ABOUT THE AUTHORS

Bob Eckstein is a *New York Times* bestselling author, advocate of independent bookstores (*Footnotes from World's Greatest Bookstores*), and snowman expert (*The Illustrated History of Snowman*). His cartoons have appeared in *MAD, SPY, Playboy*, and *The New Yorker* among many others, and he has been twice nominated by the National Cartoon Society as Gag Cartoonist of the Year. Eckstein teaches writing and drawing at NYU and is editor of *The Ultimate Cartoon Book* series. BobEckstein.com Twitter: @BobEckstein

Michael Shaw's cartoons have appeared in *The New Yorker* since 1999 and have a habit of going viral—appearing on an ABC news special following the World Trade Tower attack and on *60 Minutes* as one of *New Yorker* cartoon editor Bob Mankoff's "top five favorites." Shaw's cartoon on The Charlie Hebdo shooting led to his appearance on *Ronan Farrow Daily* on MSNBC. His cartoons have appeared in *The New Yorker Book of Literary Cartoons, The Complete Cartoons of The New Yorker, The Rejection Collection I and II, The New Yorker Encyclopedia of Cartoons, The Ultimate Cartoon Book* series and in *The St. Louis Post-Dispatch, Harvard Business Review* and *Prospect* magazine.

ACKNOWLEDGMENTS

In these uncertain times, we'd certainly like thank all the help, wit and wisdom from friends and colleagues: including Harry Siegel, Andy Simmons, Chris Monks, Mike Sacks, Jack Handey, Bob Mankoff, Michael Maslin, Ron Hauge, Alexander Salben, Teri Rizvi, Cassandra Lipp, Michael Gerber, Joe Dans, Keri-Rae Barnum, Joy Tutela, Ken Reid, Alex Avila, Trevor Hoey, Greg Smith, Beth Lawler, Tori Grant Welhouse, Elwyn Brooks White, William Strunk Jr. and Jennifer Shaw (who accepts Michael's stressful ways in cheerful good humor).

Special thanks to Marty Dundics and Andy Newton of Humorist Books— the standard in American immaturity. We lived up to that.

This book is dedicated to all stressors great and small.

BM

(Bob and Mike)

Made in the USA
Monee, IL
07 December 2020